Henry Kalen's
WINNIPEG

McNally
Robinson

MCNALLY ROBINSON BOOKSELLERS
Winnipeg

Printed and bound in Canada by Friesens Printing, Altona, Manitoba

Canadian Cataloguing in Publication Data

Kalen, Henry, 1928 -

Henry Kalen's Winnipeg

ISBN 0-9697523-1-8

1. Winnipeg (Man.) — Pictorial Works. I. Title. II. Title: Winnipeg.

FC3396.37.K34 2000   971.27'4303'0222   C00-900918-3
F1064.5.W7K34 2000

Winnipeg's distinguished architecture and varied landscape are too little known. From the late Victorian buildings of the Warehouse District to the winding banks of the Red and the Assiniboine, it is a city of unexpected vintage and variety. The oldest city in Western Canada, it offers an assortment of historic sites, urban attractions, handsome neighbourhoods and splendid parklands under a huge prairie sky. It is a city that refutes its own stereotypes. It surprises many visitors.

Winnipeg is at the confluence of two great prairie rivers, converging here before their short run to the huge inland sea of Lake Winnipeg, emptying in turn into Hudson Bay. River transportation made Winnipeg a meeting place for aboriginal tribes and then a key centre in the fur trade; the arrival of the railway at this node of activity initiated a period of political conflict, sudden wealth and dramatic growth before and after 1900. This period of upheaval was followed by relative stability and modest growth throughout the rest of the 20th century. Winnipeg's rich architectural heritage testifies to this history.

No one is better suited to capture Winnipeg on camera than Henry Kalen. He graduated as an architect from the University of Manitoba in 1957, practiced for three years and then taught at the University of Manitoba through the 1960s before finally devoting himself full time to the art of photography. The discipline of his architectural training may partly explain why, as a photographer, he is a superb technician. It surely helps explain why he has such an eye for the architectural treasures of his city.

Henry Kalen's work balances art and technique. For decades his photography has been a staple of the travel industry in Manitoba, widely reproduced in books, calendars, posters, postcards and multi-media. Tourism Winnipeg has held a poster competition each year for ten years and Henry Kalen has won it 7 times: his images have become icons of Winnipeg's consciousness. There are two explanations for this phenomenal success. One is talent: no one better appreciates the infinite variety of light and shade on a cityscape. The other is hard work: the business of being in the right place at the right time, no matter how long it takes and how much inconvenience it entails. Henry Kalen has climbed high and waited patiently for his amazing images. This book is equally a tribute to the photographer and to his city.

— Paul McNally

Downtown Winnipeg from the east, looking across the Red River and the urban forest of established residential districts in St. Boniface.

The National Bank Building is a striking example of Winnipeg's wealth of heritage architecture.

McDermot Avenue in the Exchange District, sought after for movie locations, is lined with turn-of-the century buildings.

The St. Boniface Museum with its statue of Louis Riel—statesman, rebel, martyr— is a reminder of Manitoba's turbulent entry into Canadian federation.

Riel House, on the bank of the Red River, is now surrounded by unremarkable suburban housing but is preserved as a National Historic Park.

Overleaf: Canwest Global Ballpark is situated just north of the popular recreational land of the Forks. Home to the Goldeyes of the Northern League, the park is a new addition to downtown Winnipeg.

Some of the earliest European contact with Manitoba, by the Crown-chartered Hudson's Bay Company, was by sailing ship in 1668. This two-masted replica, the Nonsuch, retraced the original journey in 1970, then took up a permanent home in its own gallery at the Manitoba Museum of Man and Nature. The Museum is a three-star attraction in the Michelin Guide to Canada.

Main Street just north of Portage Avenue is lined with civic treasures: Pantages Playhouse, the Centennial Concert Hall, the Manitoba Museum of Man and Nature and Planetarium, all across the street from City Hall. Nearby are Manitoba Theatre Centre, Warehouse Theatre, and a flock of restaurants and night clubs.

Begun in 1913 and completed in 1919 after a contracting scandal so serious it led to the defeat of the provincial government, the neo-classical Manitoba Legislature deserves its reputation as Canada's most handsome provincial capital building. At right, the headquarters of Great West Life, cornerstone among Winnipeg's corporate head offices.

The Golden Boy atop the Legislature dome was a gift from France. It spent years in transit—in cargo holds and warehouses—because of World War I shipping disruptions before reaching Winnipeg in time for the completion of the building.

Right: The opulent chamber of the Legislature.

Before the coming of the railroad, Winnipeg was linked by its rivers and it was by river that the first locomotives arrived from the south. Once the railway was established, however, the rivers declined in importance. Today the downtown rivers have been rediscovered by Winnipeggers along immensely popular riverbank walkways.

21

Traffic on the Red and Assiniboine Rivers is
now exclusively recreational. Shown here is
the Redboine Dock at sunset.

River access continues year round for cross-country skiers,
and, with the benefit of cleared trails like this one, for skaters.

The riverbank steps at the Manitoba Legislature are
the western end of the riverwalk to the Forks,
where the Assiniboine and the Red Rivers meet.

The land at the confluence of the Red and the Assiniboine, known as The Forks, was occupied for almost a century by one of Canada's major railyards. Now the old railway stable is a popular market with several restaurants.

Right: The Forks Marina and steps leading to the Plaza and Market have become, in a few short years, icons of Winnipeg and popular meeting places.

The Assiniboine River bank west of the Forks.

Approaching the Manitoba Legislature from the river side. This heroic statue of Riel was commissioned to replace a more abstract monument that portrayed a tormented soul at the end of his life.

The south façade of the Manitoba
Legislative Building.

Harbourview, in the city's northeast corner, is a successful reclamation of space long used for landfill.

Winnipeg is blessed with huge areas of urban parkland. One of the largest and best-loved parks is St. Vital Park, shown in autumn.

Inside The Conservatory, Assiniboine Park.

Assiniboine Park, Winnipeg's largest, was once controversial for being a long way from downtown. Today it is embraced by the enlarged city both literally and figuratively.

The English Gardens at Assiniboine Park. The park also encompasses attractions including the city zoo, a popular new bandshell and a miniature steam train circuit.

Cricket at Assiniboine Park. The Pavilion in the background is a Winnipeg landmark. Today it houses a restaurant and an art gallery.

A Gallery at the Sculpture Garden houses Leo Mol's smaller pieces and his drawings.

The Sculpture Garden at Assiniboine Park displays a spectacular gift: dozens of bronze statues presented to the city by Winnipeg's most famous sculptor, Leo Mol.

Sometimes known as Canada's coldest corner, Portage and Main has been famous for over a century. Today it is the focus of Winnipeg's tallest buildings.

Portage and Main skyline from the Forks.

Portage Avenue was reportedly built wide because ox carts heading west from the Red River Settlement spread across the prairie to avoid muddy ruts left by earlier traffic.

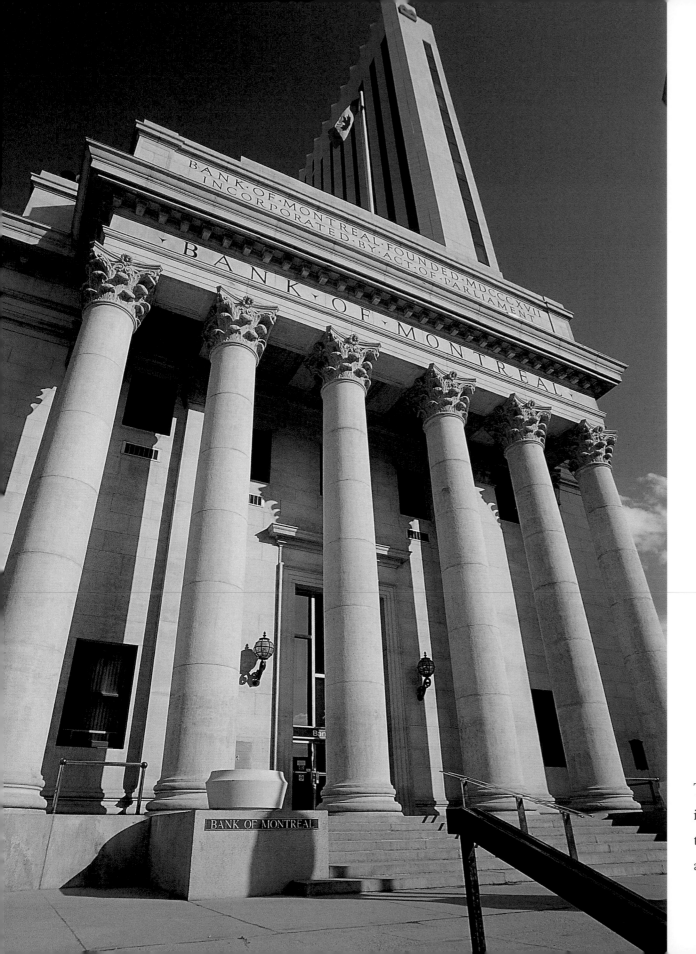

The Bank of Montreal, with its imperial classical revival façade, is the only original building remaining at Portage and Main.

The upstart new buildings of Portage and Main, viewed
from behind the columns of the Bank of Montreal.

In 1908, Emily Margaret Waddell left a bequest to the city to be paid if her husband should ever re-marry. He did. In this photograph a winter ice storm crystallizes the beauty of the Waddell Fountain in Central Park, built with the money he forfeited for love.

Today's austere City Hall replaced a grandiose romantic building which proved, alas, to be a structural folly.

Carved out of urban blight in the mid-1980s, Portage Place Mall is a grandly-conceived downtown development that houses (in addition to stores and restaurants) Prairie Theatre Exchange and cinemas, including an Imax theatre.

The first railway locomotive in Western Canada, The Countess of Dufferin, arrived by river steamer in 1877. It has been restored and is on display at Union Station. A slightly less ancient steam locomotive powers Prairie Dog Central, shown above. It is a tourist excursion train comprising several vintage rail cars that makes short scheduled trips during the summer months.

The importance of the railways to Winnipeg's early growth cannot be overestimated. The grand Fort Garry Hotel (centre) is an example of Canada's chateau-style railway hotels. To the far left, Union Station (now VIA Rail); behind, the latter-day Fort Garry Place, a large-scale inspiration in local Tyndall limestone.

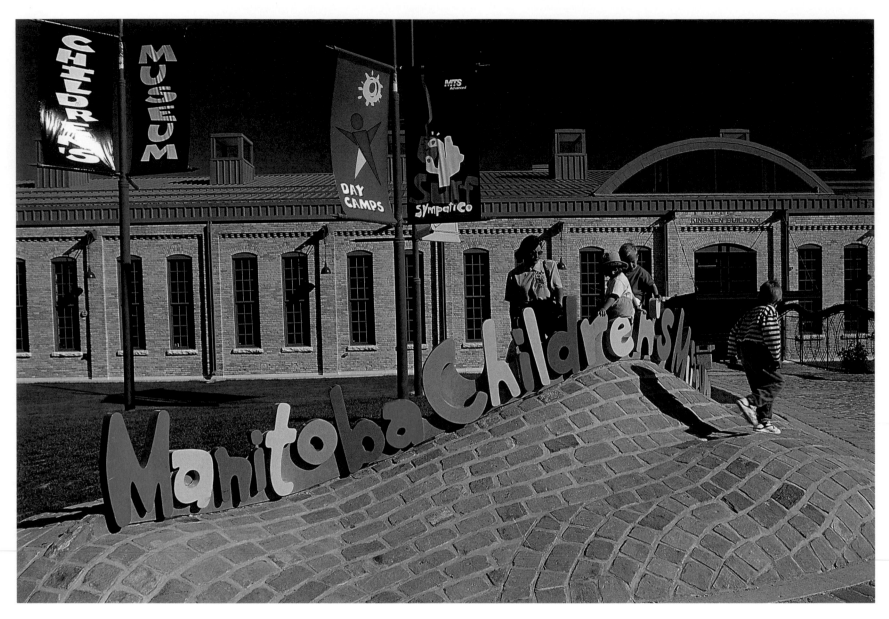

The Children's Museum at the Forks. Built in an old railway workshop,
the museum contains among many hands-on exhibits a railway gallery that
evokes the early years of Winnipeg's growth.

Fireworks
at the Forks.

The Forks National Historic Park recognizes the remarkable ancient cultures of the plains tribes who have gathered for millennia at the confluence of the Red and Assiniboine rivers. This monument is by St. Boniface sculptor Marcel Gosselin is called The Path of Time.

Oodena ("meeting place") is an amphitheatre by the Red River at the Forks National Park.

Lower Fort Garry is perhaps the most comprehensive layman's introduction to the fur trade. A national historic site, Lower Fort Garry recreates 19th century life in half a dozen buildings restored to their original functions or housing artifacts of the fur trade.

All that remains of the original Upper Fort Garry in downtown Winnipeg, far upstream from Lower Fort Garry, is this stone gate.

St. Andrews Anglican Church on River Road, towards Lower Fort
Garry and Lockport, is western Canada's oldest stone church.

The Kennedy House on River Road is a charming piece of historical preservation, comprising attractive gardens and a sunny tea room.

Lockport, with a dam and lock which control the flow of the Red River into Lake Winnipeg north of the city, draws anglers from near and far to fish for channel catfish.

One of Winnipeg's earliest industries was milling grain. Cuthbert Grant, first leader of the Métis, founded the first water mill, a structure that still stands on Sturgeon Creek near Portage Avenue.

Dalnavert, the gracious turn-of-the-century home of a prosperous lawyer who was John A. MacDonald's son, is lovingly preserved as a museum by the Manitoba Historical Society.

Many miles of Winnipeg's residential streets were planted with elm trees. Across most of North America, Dutch Elm disease has obliterated the species, but in Winnipeg tens of thousands of trees flourish. The reason: a buffer zone of largely treeless prairie helps keep the infestation at bay.

Charles Gordon to his well-heeled neighbours in Armstrong Point, Ralph O'Connor to his adoring fans, Canada's first best-selling adventure novelist lived in this home for many years; it is now the Faculty Women's Club.

A real estate survey in 2000 found that Winnipeg's most
expensive homes are better value: specifically, US $250,000
would buy a bigger, better-appointed home in Winnipeg
than in any other city in Canada or the US.

Overleaf: The Royal Canadian Mint, where coinage is made
for Canada and other countries.

Every July, for over 25 years, the Winnipeg Folk Festival has been a mecca for performers and audiences just north of the city in Bird's Hill Park.

Folklorama is a two week festival of nations held in community centres,
school auditoriums and church halls across the city by dozens of national
communities who present folk art, music and entertainment accompanied
by traditional foods.

Overleaf: Festival du Voyageur in St. Boniface each year celebrates
the pioneering fur traders who were the first Europeans to visit, then
to settle, in the Canadian West. The Festival is renowned for snow
sculpture competitions.

Dog sled rides are part of the annual Festival du Voyageur in Whittier Park.

Dragon boat practice on the Assiniboine River at the Forks.

A city of rivers is by necessity a city of bridges. Here a newly completed span of the Red River carries the TransCanada Highway toward the heart of downtown.

The bridge at left was crowned in 1999 with a river arch sculpture, above.

Winnipeg is subject to flooding. In 1997 the city was saved by this control gate structure. It diverts excess Red River flow around the city via a massive floodway—a monumental ditch that empties downstream of the city.

Although native across all the Canadian prairie provinces, the prairie crocus is Manitoba's floral emblem.

Fort Whyte Centre, founded on reclaimed land in the south of the city, acts as a wildlife sanctuary habitat and as an immensely popular interpretive centre where Winnipeggers discover the birds, animals, plants and fishes of the prairies.

St. Boniface City Hall. Winnipeg was a collection of 16 separately governed municipalities until the unicity amalgamation in 1972. Some of the original municipalities keep their distinctive character; St. Boniface remains a markedly French community.

St. Boniface Cathedral burned in a spectacular fire in 1968. Now only the dramatic façade remains.

The past and future strength of French heritage in Manitoba is obvious in this grand building, Saint Boniface College.

University of Winnipeg is a highly-regarded undergraduate university which evolved from the church-run United College.

The University of Manitoba was an amalgamation of many colleges to create Manitoba's largest university, with professional schools including Law, Medicine, Architecture, Education and Dentistry.

Celebrated for music, theatre and ballet, Winnipeg packs halls like the Centennial Concert Hall each winter season. Many residents speculate that long winters and distance from other major cities help make the arts scene vibrant in Winnipeg.

A dynamic Tyndall-stone triangle pointing north, the Winnipeg Art Gallery houses the finest collection of Inuit art in the world.

Originally coming to western Canada as industrial labourers and railway construction workers, Chinese immigrants make up a significant cultural minority in Winnipeg and add some exotic touches to the city's architecture.

The grand heritage
buildings of
Winnipeg's heyday
are gradually finding
contemporary use.

A spectacular use of windows to define form makes the Winnipeg Remand Centre a highly-regarded architectural addition to downtown.